M000074421

THE 16-BAR
POP/ROCK AUDITION

100 HIT SONGS EXCERPTED FOR SUCCESSFUL AUDITIONS

COMPILED AND EDITED BY MICHAEL DANSICKER

ISBN 978-1-4234-6887-5

HAL•LEONARD®
CORPORATION
7777 W. BLUEMOUND RD. P.O. BOX 13819 MILWAUKEE, WI 53213

Visit Hal Leonard Online at
www.halleonard.com

CONTENTS

PREFACE

The standard "open singer's call" has become the most readily available opportunity for aspiring musical theatre actors eager to introduce their talent to the professional creative teams of Broadway and touring productions. In order to accommodate the large numbers of talented, young performers, New York casting professionals have established the 16-bar excerpt as the industry standard.

THE 16-BAR AUDITION

The selection should be no longer than thirty seconds and should clearly represent the style and spirit of the musical being cast. If the song is written in a very fast cut time, 32 bars would be appropriate. Dialects should be avoided; and unless specifically noted, the lyric should be sung in English. Your goal is to select the *best* 16 bars of the song chosen. Selecting an arbitrary 16 bars is not always useful. Because standard theatre music (written before 1970) often adheres to the 32-bar song form (AABA), it is fairly easy to excerpt and edit for audition purposes. Contemporary musical theatre writing faithfully serves the drama its writers are musicalizing but is rarely successfully consolidated for 16-bar cuttings. Keep the introduction short (a bell tone is fine) and clearly mark your music! Any transposition should be neatly written out, and original material from camp shows, revues, and your best friend's newest musical should be left at home. Indicate the tempo clearly to the accompanist.

THE CHANGING SOUND OF BROADWAY

While few songs written for new Broadway musicals have hit the record charts as viable best sellers, there has been a new addition to today's musical theatre genre. That is: The Jukebox Musical. Ticket buyers, shelling out a great deal of money for their entertainment, are often excited about hearing the old, familiar songs of beloved Pop artists showcased in a legitimate theatre vehicle. ABBA, Elvis, Green Day, The Beach Boys, Dolly Parton, Buddy Holly, Bob Dylan, John Lennon, Frankie Valli, Billy Joel, Johnny Cash and Queen have all been represented in London's West End and on the Great White Way. In addition, shows based on Disney animated classics (i.e. *The Lion King*, *The Little Mermaid*, and *Mary Poppins*) and TV productions (i.e. *High School Musical 1, 2*, and *3* and *Glee*) have become part of the new tradition. The songs from Broadway properties reinvented for film (i.e. *Dreamgirls*, *Rent*, *Hairspray* and *Nine*) are now an important addition to today's audition repertory. TV's *American Idol* has introduced a new generation to the Pop music of past decades as well as the Broadway classics of yesteryear. All are approached in a contemporary, stylized way, and their impact on young performers can not be discounted. No longer can the complete musical theatre performer ignore the Pop/Rock music of the last fifty years. It is now a living part of the Broadway Songbook. The audition landscape has changed, but good singing technique and vocal discipline are invaluable in successfully utilizing this material for auditions.

THE CHALLENGE

Music created and recorded by popular artists has the advantage of being produced in a recording studio. Background vocals and intricate programmed drums/sequenced synth tracks are as much a part of the fabric of the song as the actual music and lyric. Obviously, the accompaniment of a theatre audition pianist will never evoke the punch and fill of a produced musical orchestration. However, stripping the song down to basic elements can be an advantage. While the dramatic element of a true theatre song is ultimately more specific in intention and ultimate performance, many Pop songs have a winning simplicity and strong emotional line. It is up to the performer to choose how far the dramatic context of the song can be developed and to decide how far the vocal envelope can be exploited at an audition. But total commitment to your work as actor and singer is imperative. Don't forget to impart the joy of being a musical theatre actor.

VOCAL RANGES

You can't show everything in 16 bars! Your audition is an introduction of your vocal and acting expertise to a production team. I have never approved of interpolated high notes in 16-bar selections. A note inserted to show range, with no cohesive relation to the phrase, will not work favorably for you. However, the transposition of a selection to a place in your voice that is exciting and attractive is standard procedure. Remember, the upper limits of range are "the norm" in today's commercial market. It is not unusual to expect ladies to belt an E5. Baritones are requested to sing G5, and many tenors are required to have a high C6. It is a world of "higher and louder!" And legit sopranos must have the courage to tackle material outside of the standard musical theatre rep.

SELECTIONS IN THESE VOLUMES

I have attempted to include a wide variety of composition and style in these volumes. It should never be the intention of any actor to mimic a particular artist. Work with the lyric and the musical setting to create your own take on the material. I know you will find that these songs are worth investigating in a dramatic context. Don't be afraid to use a song that is used often at auditions. The creative team is looking for your "take" on the material. Every actor is unique, and your understanding of a song that is commonly sung just might be that special something that gets you a callback.

LESS THAN 16 BARS

Many casting directors in New York/L.A. auditions have scaled back the 16-bar standard cutting to 8 bars in order to accommodate the large number of singers attending various calls. Of course, limiting a performance to 8 bars tends to strip the dramatic integrity from the audition! However, an experienced creative team will certainly note your accuracy of pitch and placement. Your negotiating a song's range and phrasing challenges can also be determined in a shortened audition cutting.

BE PREPARED!

It is very important that if a 16-bar selection becomes a part of your audition book that you also take the time to learn and master the entire piece. There is always the chance a director will say: "That was sensational! Let's hear the whole song!"

Michael Dansicker
New York City
May, 2010

MICHAEL DANSICKER has worked as arranger, composer, musical director and pianist on over 100 Broadway and Off-Broadway productions. He wrote the dance and incidental music for Rachel Portman's *Little House on the Prairie* (starring Melissa Gilbert) and the songs for Jim Davis's *Garfield Live* (with Bill Meade). Last season, he arranged, scored, and supervised Bob Dylan and Twyla Tharp's *The Times They Are a Changin'*. His new musical *Shooting Star: The Bobby Driscoll Story* (directed by Francesca Zambello) is currently in development. He served as vocal consultant to the hit films: *Elf* (New Line Cinema), *Analyze That* (WB), *Meet the Parents* (Universal) and scored the dances for Paramount's *Brain Donors*. In the world of Concert Dance: ABT, Twyla Tharp, Agnes de Mille, JOFFREY, Jerome Robbins, Donald McKayle, Geoffrey Holder, Mikhail Baryshnikov and Kenny Ortega. He has worked as creative consultant to Walt Disney Entertainment and is one of the country's leading vocal specialists and session pianists.

Special thanks to Rick Walters at Hal Leonard, Fran Charnas (Boston Conservatory), Scot Reese and Carmen Balthrop (University of Maryland), Clay James (Montclair State University), Michael Cassara, and the "Dean" of Broadway Casting – JAY BINDER!

AGAINST ALL ODDS
(Take a Look at Me Now)
from *Against All Odds*
recorded by Phil Collins
excerpt

Words and Music by
PHIL COLLINS

ALL BY MYSELF
recorded by Celine Dion
excerpt

Music by SERGEI RACHMANINOFF
Words and Additional Music by ERIC CARMEN

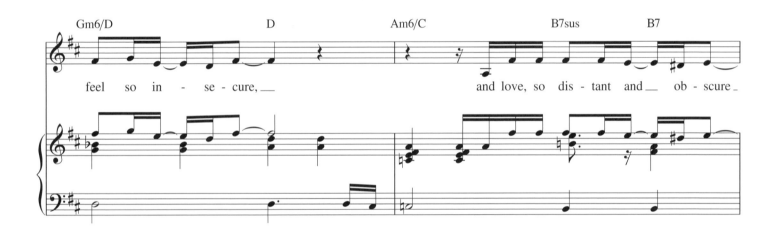

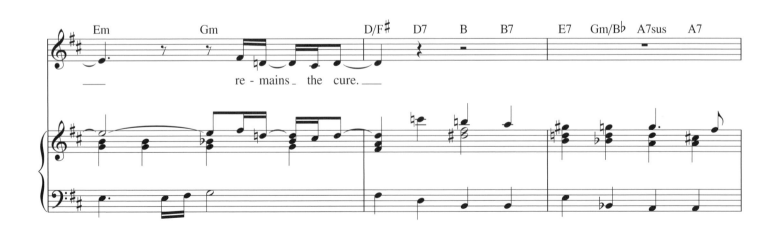

ALL I NEED
recorded by Jack Wagner

excerpt

Words and Music by DAVID PACK,
GLEN BALLARD and CLIF MAGNESS

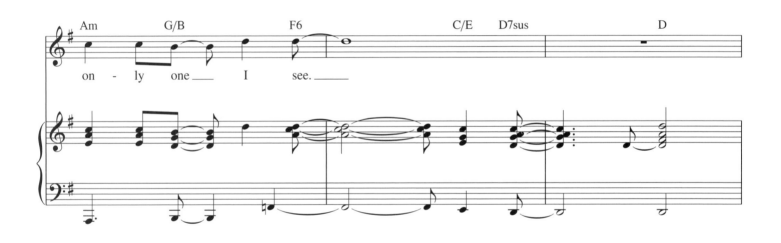

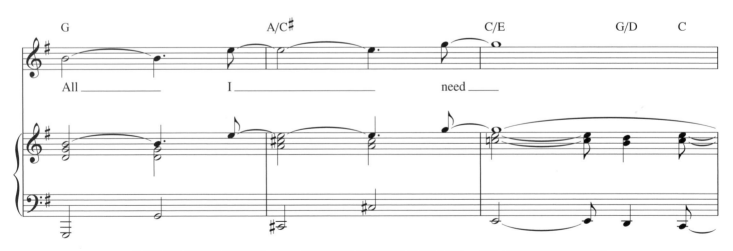

ALL MY LOVING
recorded by The Beatles
excerpt

Words and Music by JOHN LENNON
and PAUL McCARTNEY

Moderately fast, with a Swing feel

Close your eyes and I'll kiss you, to-mor-row I'll miss you; re-mem-ber I'll al-ways be true. And then while I'm a-way, I'll write home ev-'ry day and I'll send all my lov-ing to you.

BABY I NEED YOUR LOVIN'

recorded by Johnny Rivers; The Four Tops

excerpt

Words and Music by BRIAN HOLLAND,
LAMONT DOZIER and EDWARD HOLLAND

AMANDA
recorded by Boston
excerpt

Words and Music by
TOM SCHOLZ

BACK TO YOU
recorded by Bryan Adams
excerpt

Words and Music by BRYAN ADAMS
and ELIOT KENNEDY

Lively Rock

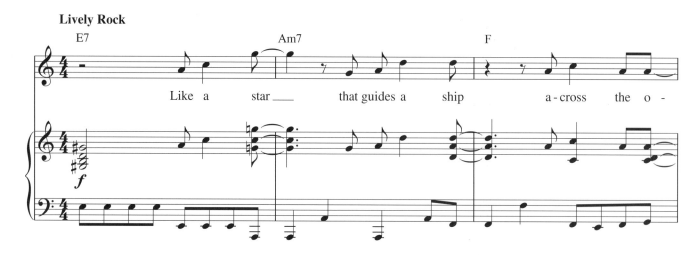

Like a star ___ that guides a ship a-cross the o-

- cean, that's how your love can take me home

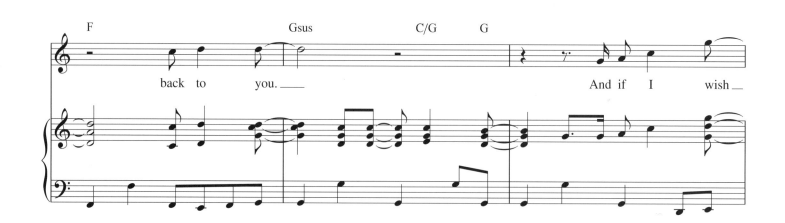

back to you. ___ And if I wish ___

BEST OF MY LOVE
recorded by The Eagles

excerpt

Words and Music by JOHN DAVID SOUTHER,
DON HENLEY and GLENN FREY

COME TOGETHER
recorded by The Beatles
excerpt

Words and Music by JOHN LENNON
and PAUL McCARTNEY

BLAZE OF GLORY
featured in the film *Young Guns II*
recorded by Bon Jovi
excerpt

Words and Music by
JON BON JOVI

Moderate Rock

BREAKING FREE

from the Disney Channel Original Movie *High School Musical*
recorded by Zac Efron & Vanessa Anne Hudgens

excerpt

Words and Music by
JAMIE HOUSTON

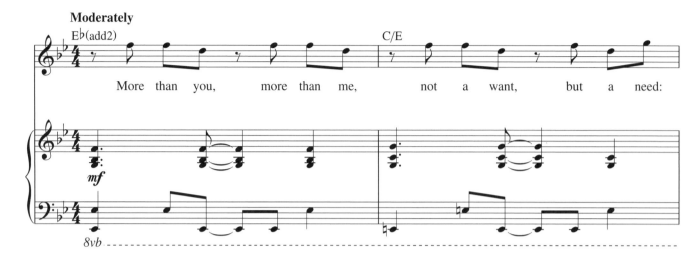

More than you, more than me, not a want, but a need:

both of us break-in' free. ____

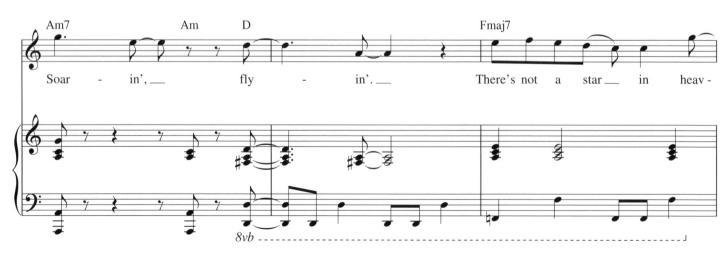

Soar - in', ____ fly - in'. ____ There's not a star in heav-

BREAKING UP IS HARD TO DO

recorded by Neil Sedaka

excerpt

Words and Music by HOWARD GREENFIELD
and NEIL SEDAKA

Slowly

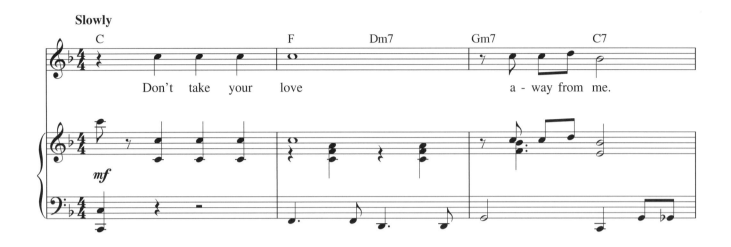

Don't take your love a-way from me.

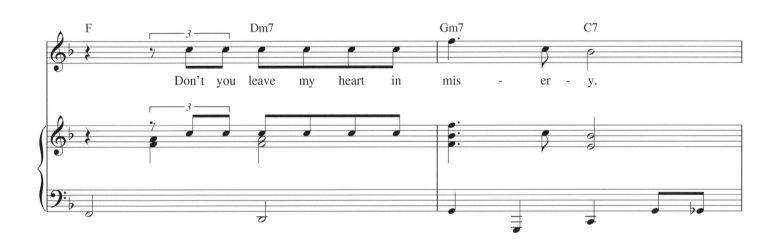

Don't you leave my heart in mis - er - y.

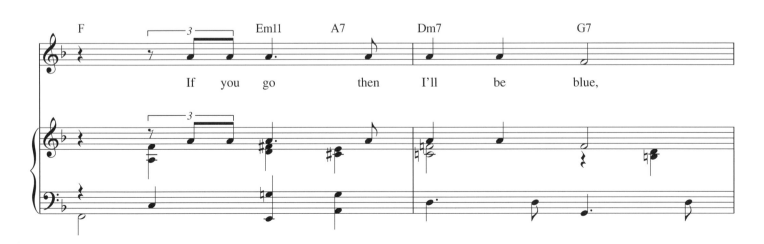

If you go then I'll be blue,

BUT IT'S ALRIGHT

recorded by J.J. Jackson; Huey Lewis & The News

excerpt

Words and Music by JEROME L. JACKSON
and PIERRE TUBBS

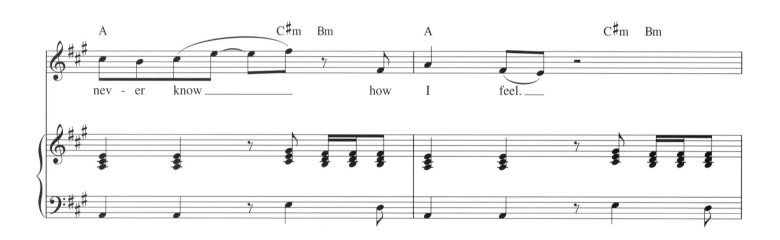

CAN'T BUY ME LOVE

recorded by The Beatles

excerpt

Words and Music by JOHN LENNON
and PAUL McCARTNEY

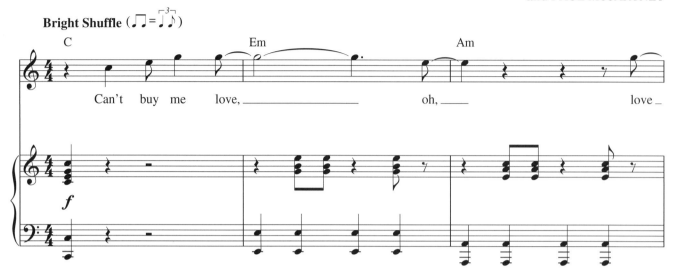

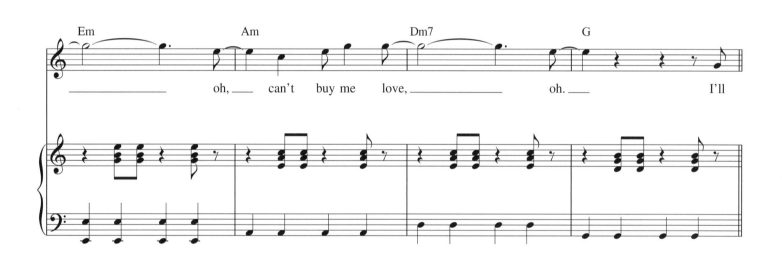

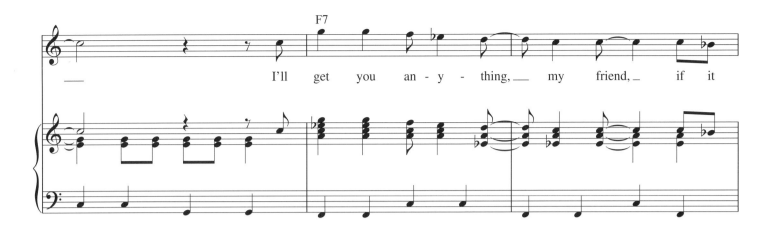

I'll get you an-y-thing, __ my friend, __ if it

makes you feel al - right. __ 'Cause I don't care too

much for mon - ey, for mon - ey can't buy me love. __

CAN'T TAKE MY EYES OFF OF YOU

recorded by Frankie Valli & The Four Seasons

excerpt

Words and Music by
BOB CREWE and BOB GAUDIO

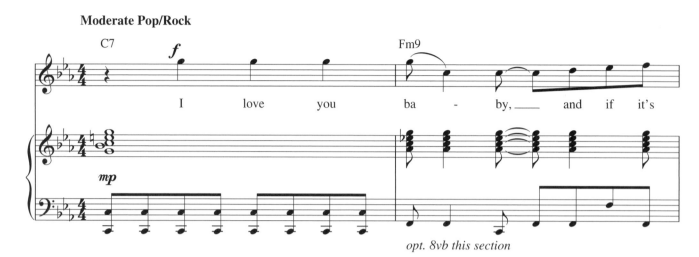

COME AND GET IT

recorded by Badfinger

excerpt

Words and Music by
PAUL McCARTNEY

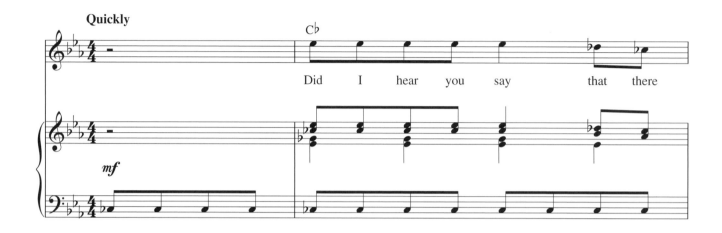

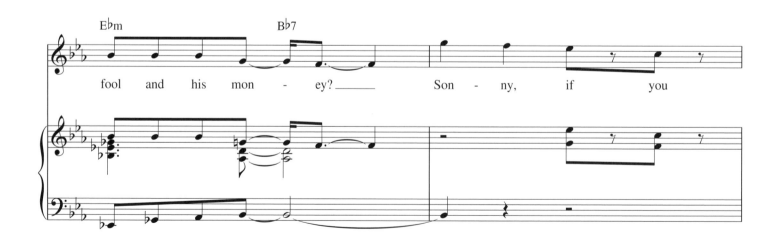

CRAZY LITTLE THING CALLED LOVE

recorded by Queen

excerpt

Words and Music by
FREDDIE MERCURY

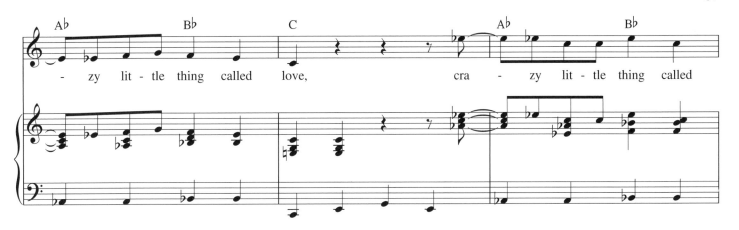

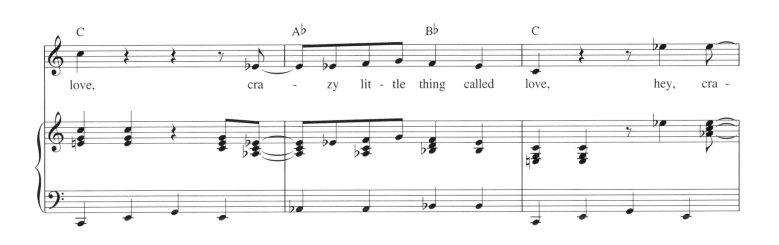

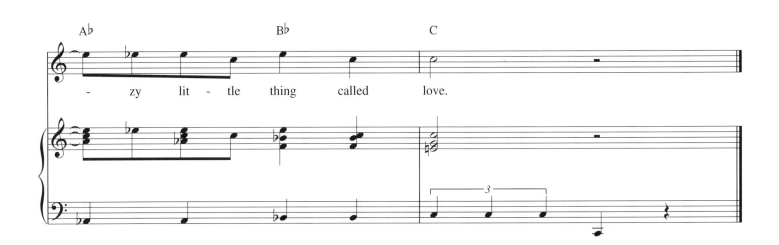

CROCODILE ROCK
recorded by Elton John
excerpt

Words and Music by ELTON JOHN
and BERNIE TAUPIN

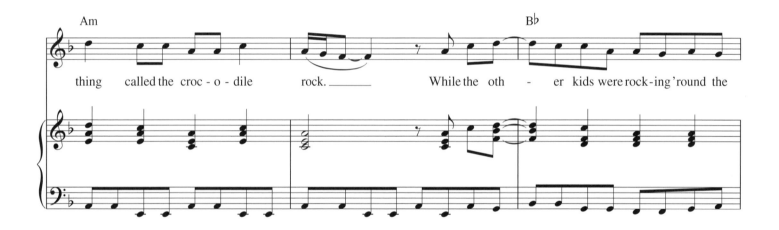

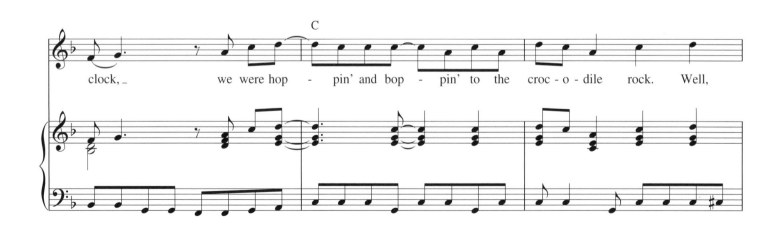

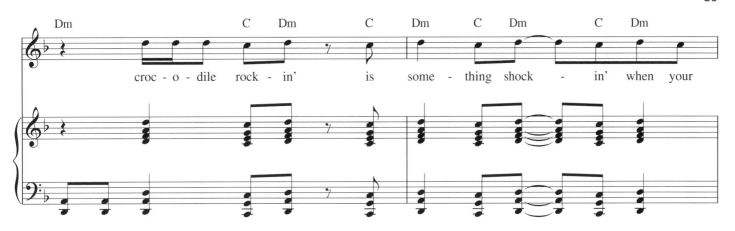

DANCE TONIGHT

recorded by Paul McCartney

excerpt

Words and Music by
PAUL McCARTNEY

Ev-'ry-bod-y gon-na dance to-night, __ ev-'ry-bod-y gon-na feel al - right,

ev-'ry-bod - y gon-na dance a - round __ to - night. __

Ev-'ry-bod-y gon-na dance a - round, __ ev-'ry-bod - y gon-na hit the ground, __

ev-'ry-bod-y gon-na dance a - round _ to - night. __

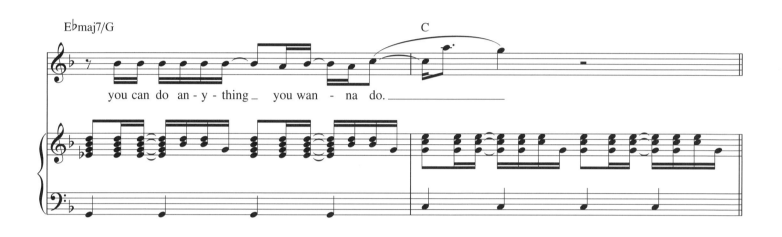

DOIN' IT
(All for My Baby)
recorded by Huey Lewis & The News
excerpt

Words and Music by PHIL CODY
and MIKE DUKE

FIELDS OF GOLD
recorded by Sting

excerpt

Music and Lyrics by
STING

DON'T LET THE SUN GO DOWN ON ME

recorded by Elton John

excerpt

Words and Music by ELTON JOHN
and BERNIE TAUPIN

to wan - der free. _____

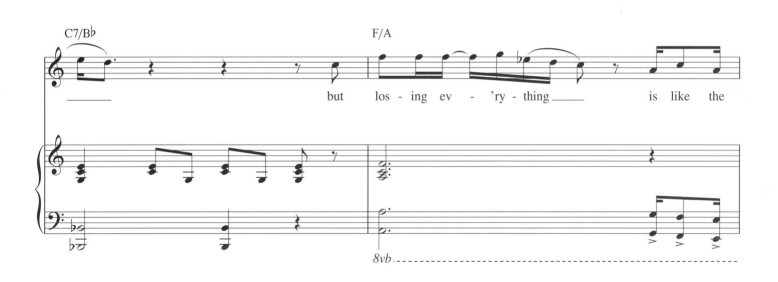

but los - ing ev - 'ry - thing _____ is like the

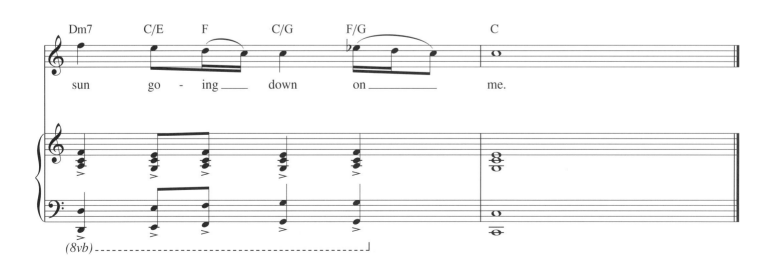

sun go - ing _____ down on _____ me.

DON'T STOP
recorded by Fleetwood Mac
excerpt

Words and Music by
CHRISTINE McVIE

Moderate Rock Shuffle

If you wake up and don't want to smile; ___

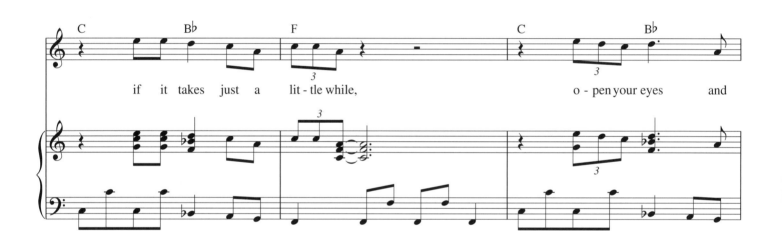

if it takes just a lit-tle while, o-pen your eyes and

look at the day. ___ You'll see things in a dif-f'rent ___ way. ___

ELEANOR RIGBY
recorded by The Beatles
excerpt

Words and Music by JOHN LENNON
and PAUL McCARTNEY

Moderately, with a steady beat

El - ea - nor Rig - by picks up the rice __ in the church __

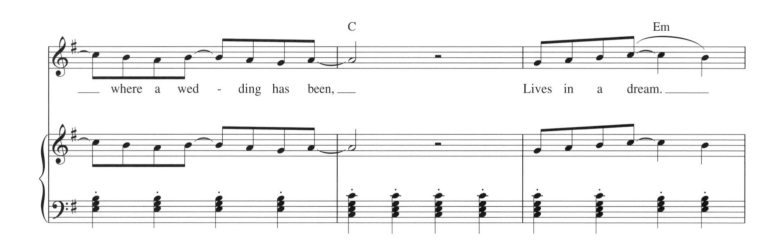

__ where a wed - ding has been, __ Lives in a dream. __

Waits at the win - dow, wear - ing the face __ that she keeps __

EVERY BREATH YOU TAKE
recorded by The Police
excerpt

Music and Lyrics by
STING

Moderate Rock

Ev-'ry move you _ make, ev-'ry vow you _

break, ev-'ry smile _ you fake, ev-'ry claim _ you stake,

I'll be watch-ing you.

EVERY LITTLE THING SHE DOES IS MAGIC

recorded by The Police
excerpt

Music and Lyrics by
STING

tried be - fore __ to tell __ her of the feel - ings I have for her in __ my __

__ heart, __ ev - 'ry time __

__ that I __ come near __ her I __ just lose __ my nerve __ as I've __ done from the start. __

EVERYTIME I CLOSE MY EYES

recorded by Babyface

excerpt

Words and Music by
BABYFACE

Moderately Slow Ballad

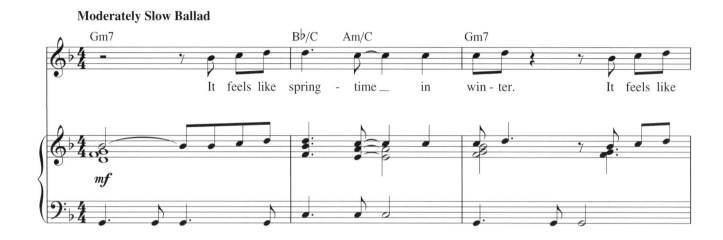

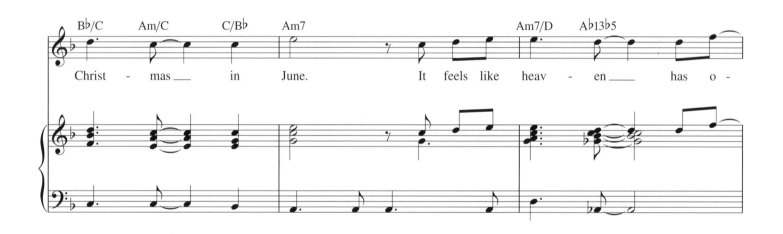

thank the Lord that I've __ got you __ and you've got me, too. __ And

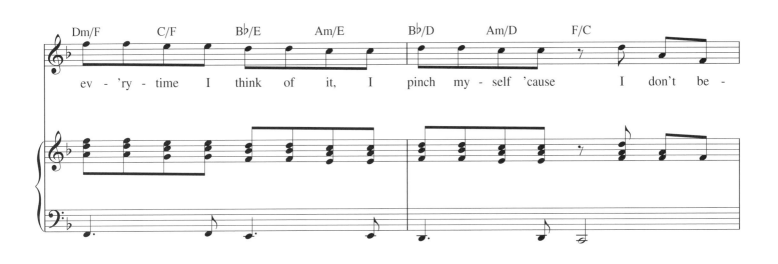

ev - 'ry - time I think of it, I pinch my - self 'cause I don't be -

lieve it's true that some - one like you __ loves __ me too.

FORTRESS AROUND YOUR HEART

recorded by Sting

excerpt

Music and Lyrics by
STING

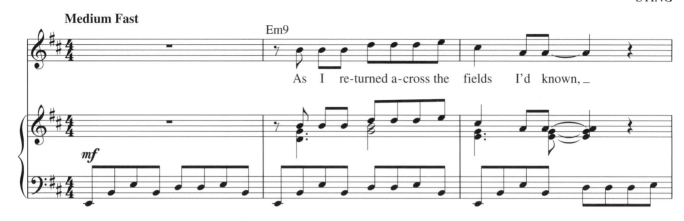

As I re-turned a-cross the fields I'd known, __

I rec-og-nized __ the walls that I once made. __ Had to stop in my tracks for fear __ of

walk-ing on __ the mines __ I'd laid. And if _____ I've built __ this for - tress __ a-

round your heart, en - cir-cled you __ in trench - es and __ barbed wire.

HE AIN'T HEAVY, HE'S MY BROTHER

recorded by The Hollies; Neil Diamond

excerpt

Words and Music by BOB RUSSELL
and BOBBY SCOTT

GOLDEN SLUMBERS

recorded by The Beatles

excerpt

Words and Music by JOHN LENNON
and PAUL McCARTNEY

Sleep, pret-ty dar - ling, do not cry,

and I will sing a lull-a - by. _____

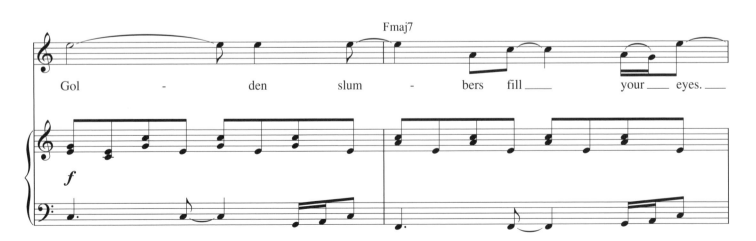

Gol - den slum - bers fill ___ your ___ eyes. ___

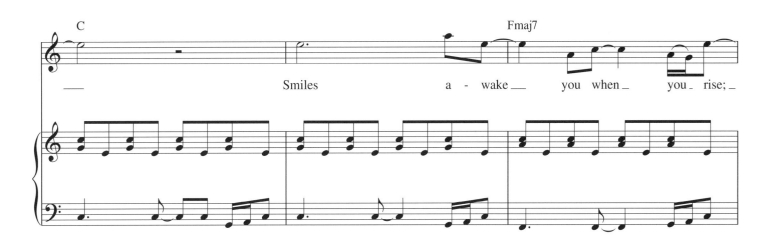

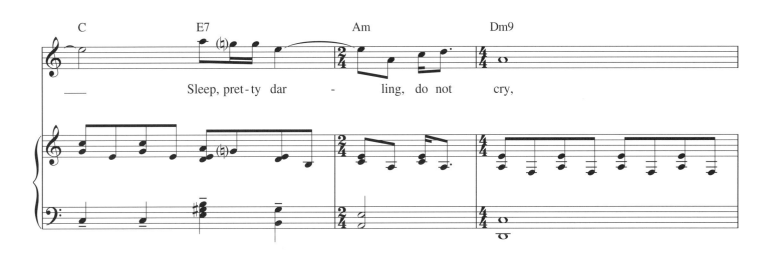

HERE, THERE AND EVERYWHERE

recorded by The Beatles

excerpt

Words and Music by JOHN LENNON
and PAUL McCARTNEY

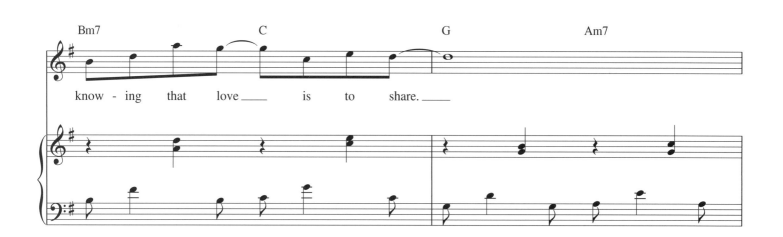

HERO

recorded by Mariah Carey

excerpt

Words and Music by MARIAH CAREY
and WALTER AFANASIEFF

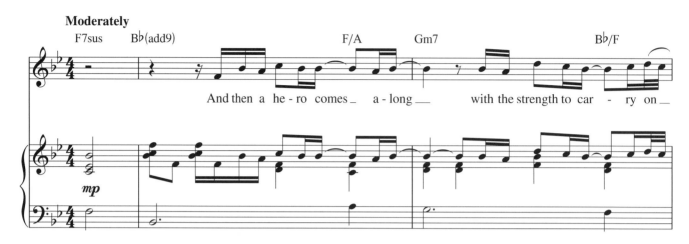

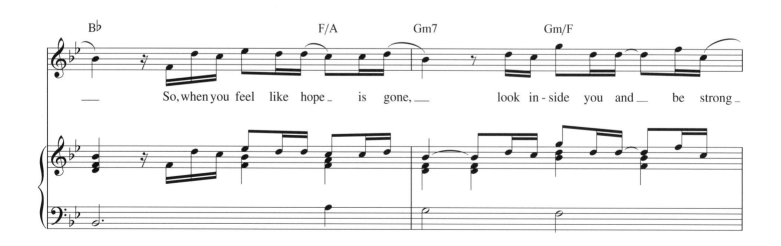

and you'll fi - n'ly see __ the truth __ that a he - ro lies __ in you. __

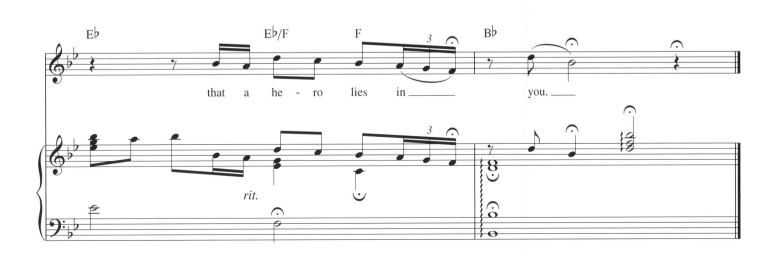

that a he - ro lies in __ you. __

HIGHER GROUND

recorded by Stevie Wonder; Red Hot Chili Peppers

excerpt

Words and Music by
STEVIE WONDER

Fast Bluesy Rock

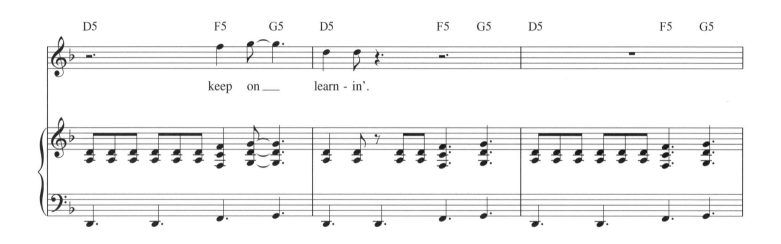

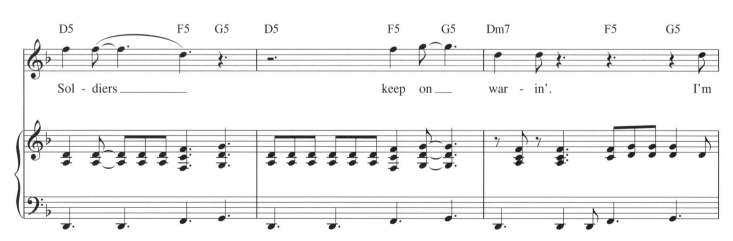

HIT ME WITH YOUR BEST SHOT
recorded by Pat Benatar
excerpt

Words and Music by
EDDIE SCHWARTZ

Moderate Rock

Well, you're a real tough cook - ie with a

long his - to - ry of break-ing lit - tle hearts like the one in me.

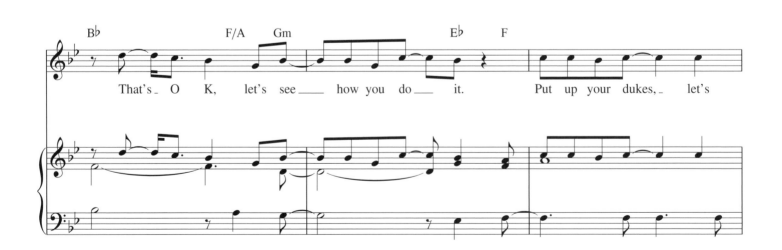

That's O K, let's see ___ how you do ___ it. Put up your dukes, ___ let's

HOME
recorded by Daughtry
excerpt

Words and Music by
CHRIS DAUGHTRY

Oh _____ well, I'm go - in' home, _____ back to the place where I _____ be - long _____ and where your love has al - ways been e - nough _ for me. _____ I'm not run - nin' from, _____ no, I think you got _ me all _____ wrong. _ I don't re - gret _ this life _____ I chose _ for me. _

70

HONESTY
recorded by Billy Joel
excerpt

Words and Music by
BILLY JOEL

Slowly (♩ = 66)

If you __ search for ten - der - ness __ it is - n't hard to find. __ You can have __ the love __ you need __ to live, __ but if you __ look for truth - ful - ness __ you might just as well __ be blind; __ it al - ways seems to be so hard __ to give.

© 1978 IMPULSIVE MUSIC
All Rights Reserved   International Copyright Secured   Used by Permission

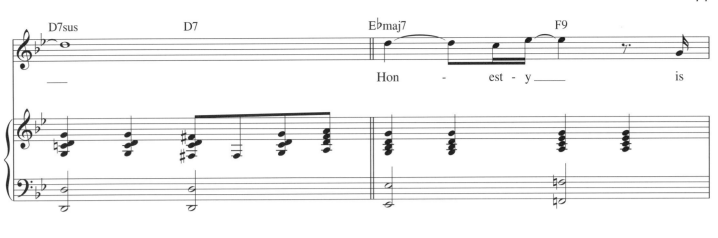

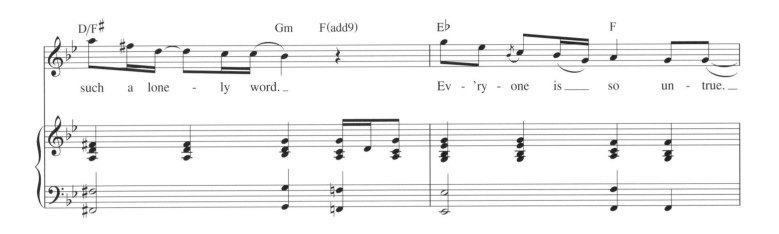

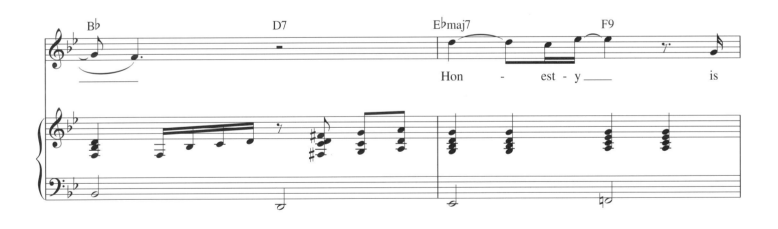

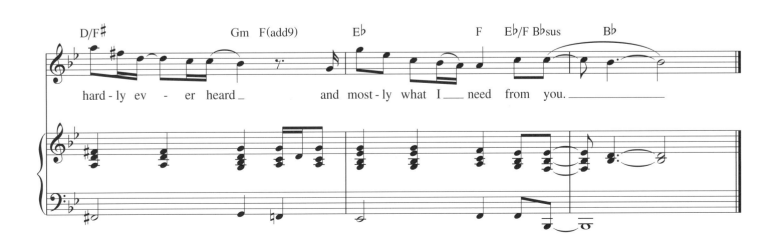

HOW AM I SUPPOSED TO LIVE WITHOUT YOU

recorded by Michael Bolton

excerpt

Words and Music by MICHAEL BOLTON
and DOUG JAMES

So tell me all a-bout it, tell me 'bout the plans you're mak-

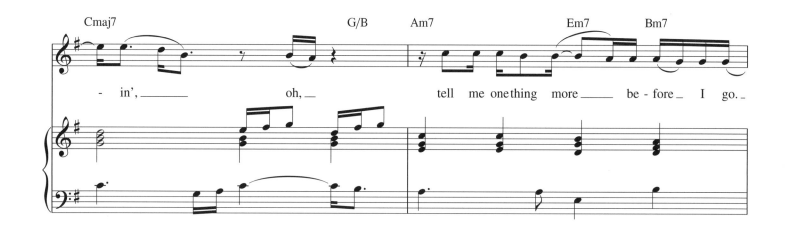

-in', _____ oh, _____ tell me one thing more _____ be-fore _ I go. _

Tell me how am I _____ sup-posed _____ to live _ with-out _

HOW SWEET IT IS
(To Be Loved by You)
recorded by Marvin Gaye; James Taylor

excerpt

Words and Music by EDWARD HOLLAND,
LAMONT DOZIER and BRIAN HOLLAND

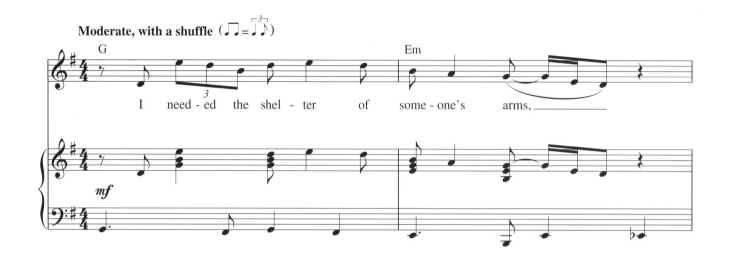

I need-ed the shel-ter of some-one's arms,

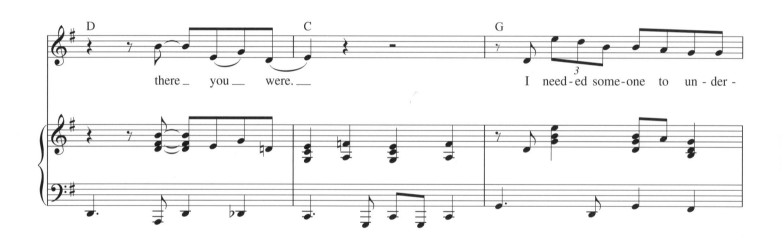

there you were. I need-ed some-one to un-der-

stand my ups and downs, there you were,

I CAN SEE FOR MILES
recorded by The Who
excerpt

Words and Music by
PETER TOWNSHEND

I'LL BE THERE

recorded by The Jackson 5; Mariah Carey

excerpt

Words and Music by BERRY GORDY, HAL DAVIS,
WILLIE HUTCH and BOB WEST

I CAN'T HELP MYSELF
(Sugar Pie, Honey Bunch)
recorded by The Four Tops

excerpt

Words and Music by BRIAN HOLLAND,
LAMONT DOZIER and EDWARD HOLLAND

(Everything I Do)
I DO IT FOR YOU

from the Motion Picture *Robin Hood: Prince of Thieves*
recorded by Bryan Adams

excerpt

Words and Music by BRYAN ADAMS,
R.J. LANGE and MICHAEL KAMEN

I NEED YOU

recorded by Marc Anthony

excerpt

Words and Music by
CORY ROONEY

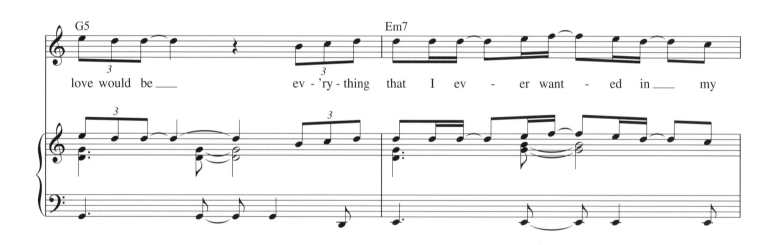

I WANT LOVE
recorded by Elton John
excerpt

Words and Music by ELTON JOHN
and BERNIE TAUPIN

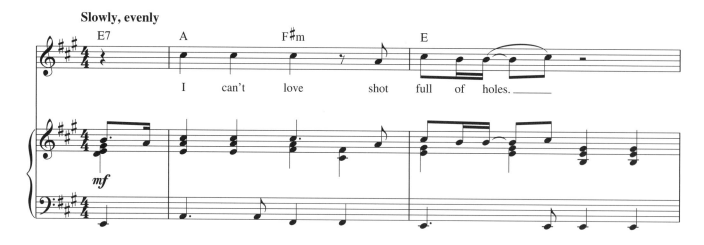

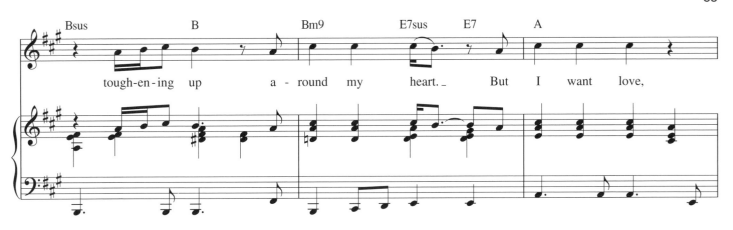

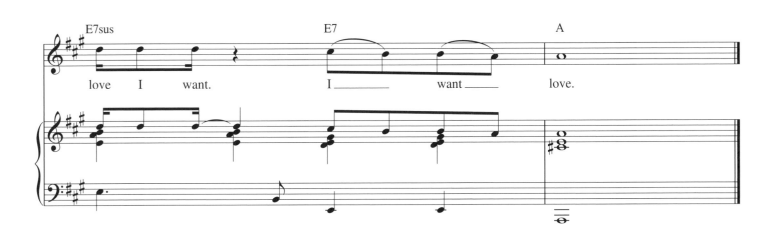

I WILL REMEMBER YOU

Theme from *The Brothers McMullen*
recorded by Sarah McLachlan
excerpt

Words and Music by SARAH McLACHLAN,
SEAMUS EGAN and DAVE MERENDA

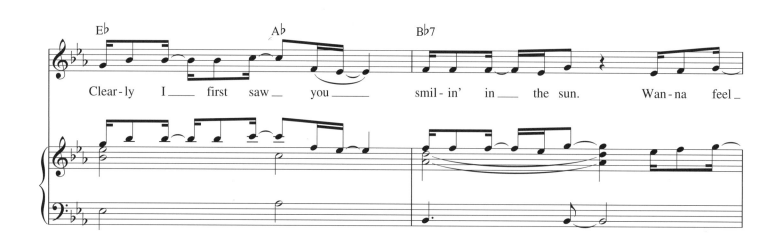

I'LL STAND BY YOU

recorded by Pretenders; Carrie Underwood

excerpt

Words and Music by CHRISSIE HYNDE,
TOM KELLY and BILLY STEINBERG

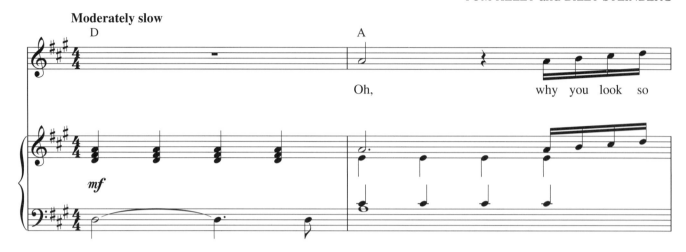

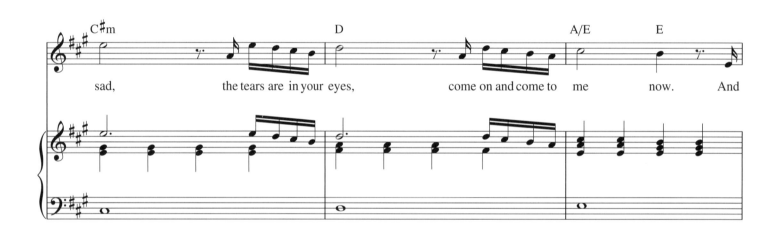

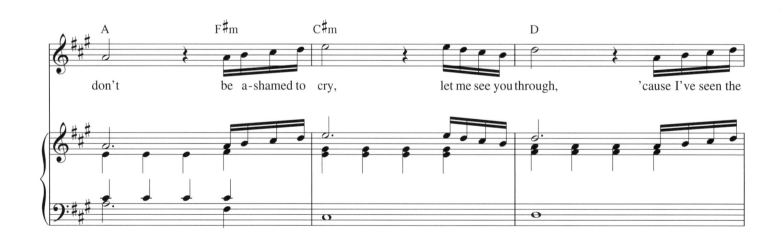

I'M A BELIEVER
recorded by The Monkees; Smash Mouth
excerpt

Words and Music by
NEIL DIAMOND

IF I FELL
recorded by The Beatles
excerpt

Words and Music by JOHN LENNON
and PAUL McCARTNEY

IF
recorded by Bread
excerpt

Words and Music by
DAVID GATES

Moderately, with feeling

If the world should stop re-volv-

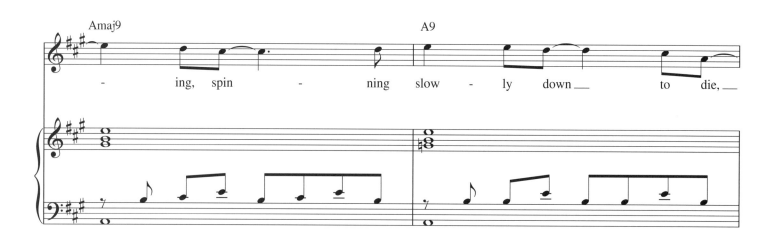

-ing, spin - ning slow - ly down ___ to die, ___

I'd spend ___ the end ___ with you; ___

IMAGINE

recorded by John Lennon

excerpt

Words and Music by
JOHN LENNON

IT'S STILL ROCK AND ROLL TO ME

recorded by Billy Joel

excerpt

Words and Music by
BILLY JOEL

Moderately fast

What's the mat - ter with the

clothes I'm wear - ing? "Can't you tell that your tie's too wide?" _

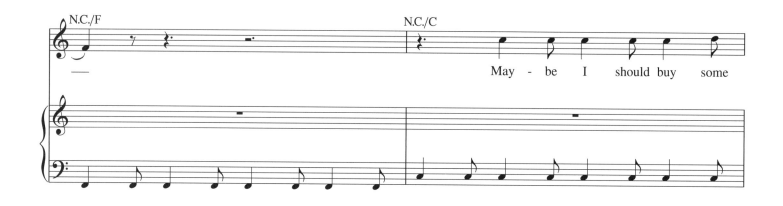

— May - be I should buy some

old tab col - lars? "Wel - come back to the age of jive. ___

JUST THE WAY YOU ARE
recorded by Billy Joel
excerpt

Words and Music by
BILLY JOEL

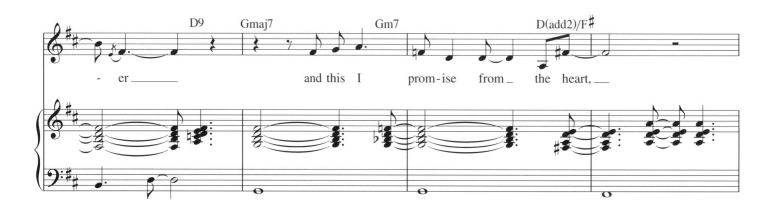

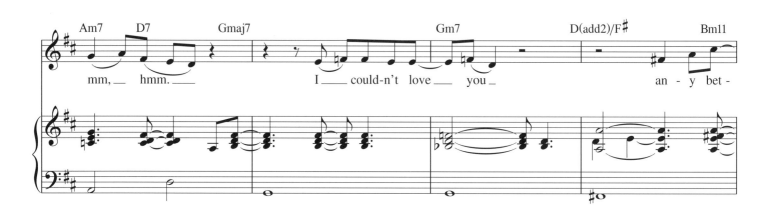

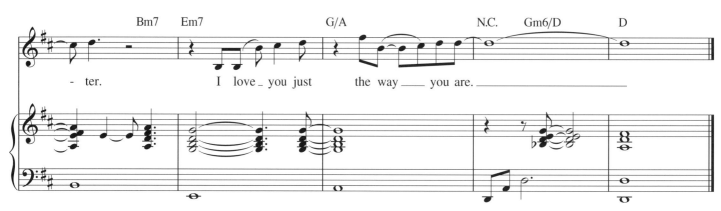

LADY
recorded by Lionel Richie
excerpt

Words and Music by
LIONEL RICHIE

KIDS WANNA ROCK

recorded by Bryan Adams

excerpt

Words and Music by BRYAN ADAMS
and JIM VALLANCE

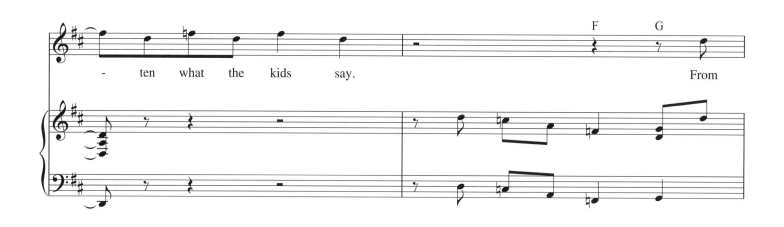

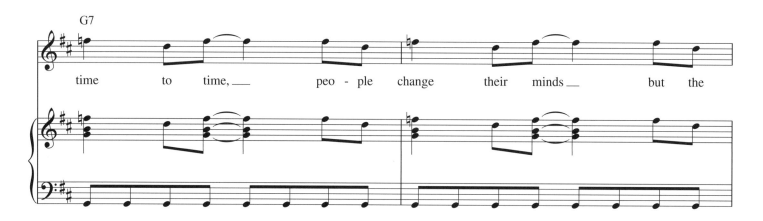

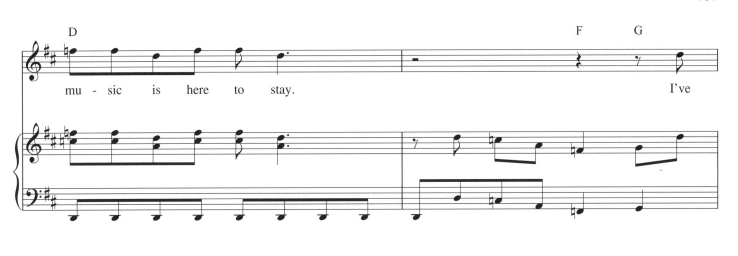

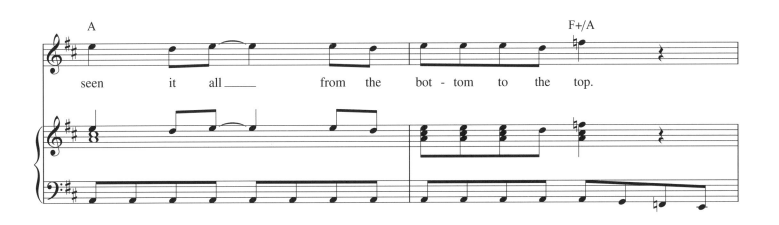

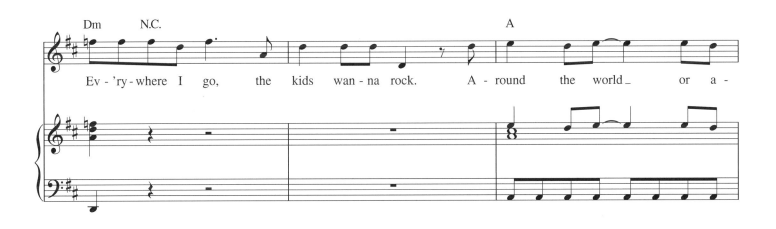

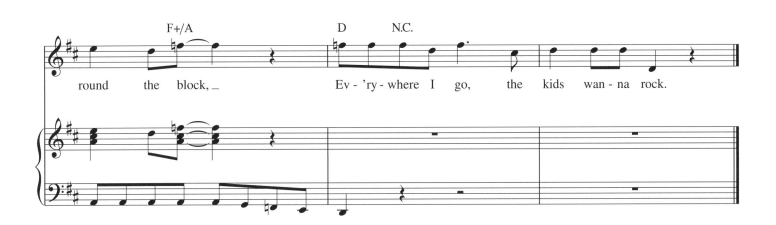

LATELY
recorded by Stevie Wonder
excerpt

Words and Music by
STEVIE WONDER

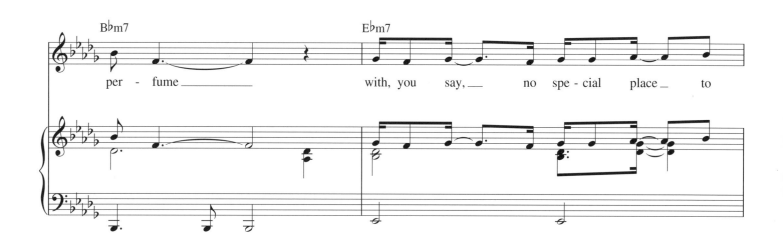

LET HER CRY
recorded by Hootie & The Blowfish
excerpt

Words and Music by DARIUS CARLOS RUCKER,
EVERETT DEAN FELBER, MARK WILLIAM BRYAN
and JAMES GEORGE SONEFELD

LET IT BE
recorded by The Beatles
excerpt

Words and Music by JOHN LENNON
and PAUL McCARTNEY

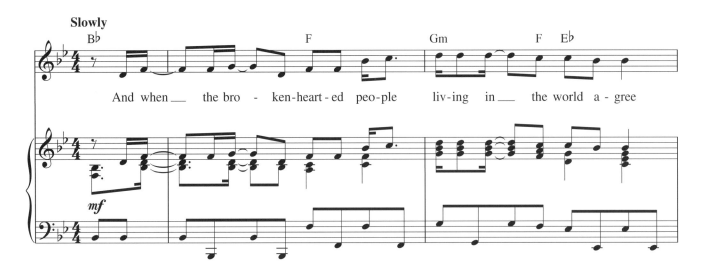

And when the bro-ken-heart-ed peo-ple liv-ing in the world a-gree

there will be an an-swer, let it be. For

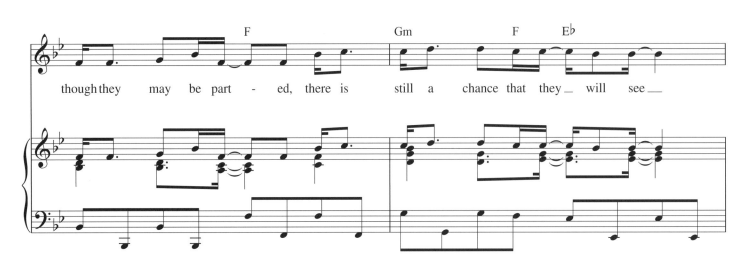

though they may be part-ed, there is still a chance that they will see

there will be an an - swer; let it be. _____ Let it be, _

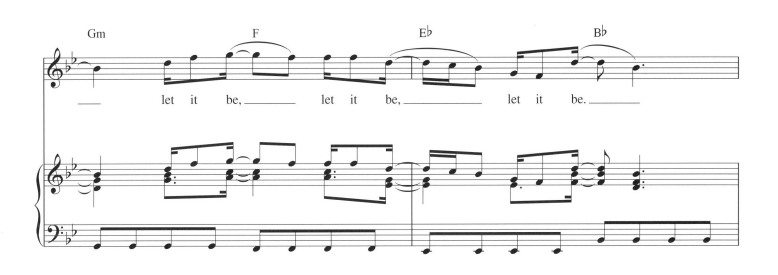

_ let it be, _____ let it be, _____ let it be.

There will be _ an an - swer; let it be. _____

LIVIN' ON A PRAYER
recorded by Bon Jovi

excerpt

Words and Music by JON BON JOVI,
DESMOND CHILD and RICHIE SAMBORA

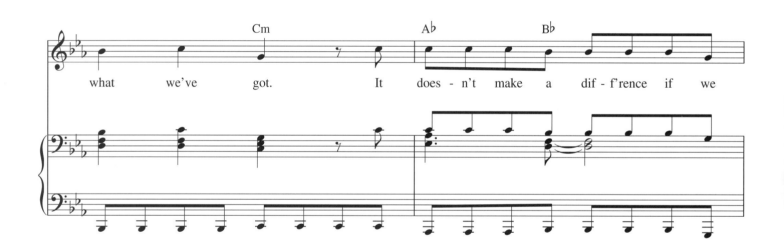

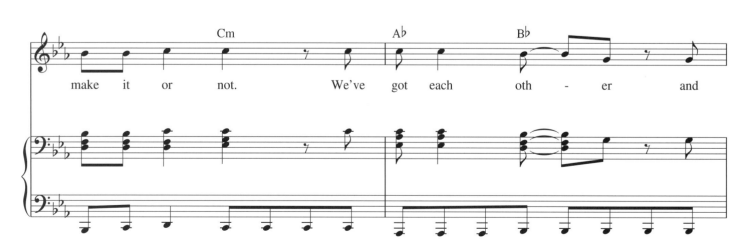

THE LONG AND WINDING ROAD

recorded by The Beatles

excerpt

Words and Music by JOHN LENNON
and PAUL McCARTNEY

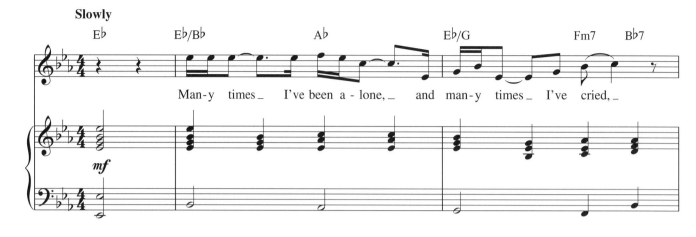

Man-y times __ I've been a-lone, __ and man-y times __ I've cried, __

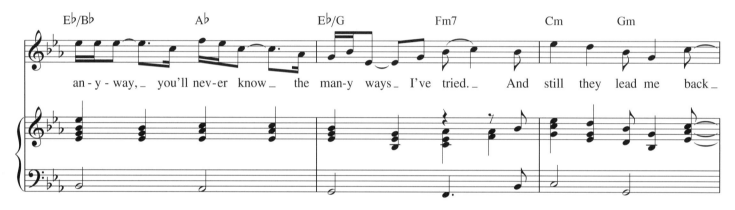

an-y-way, __ you'll nev-er know __ the man-y ways __ I've tried. And still they lead me back __

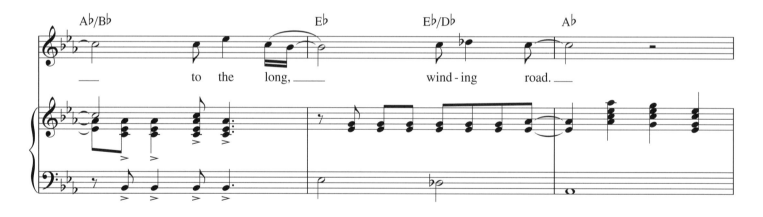

__ to the long, _____ wind-ing road. _____

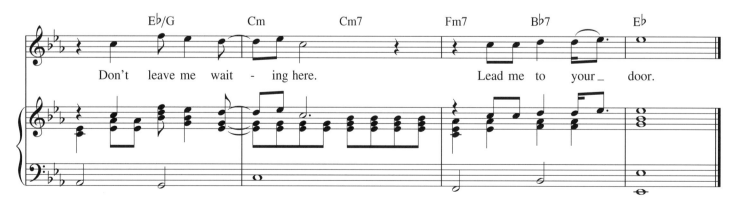

Don't leave me wait-ing here. Lead me to your __ door.

LOOKS LIKE WE MADE IT

recorded by Barry Manilow

excerpt

Words and Music by RICHARD KERR
and WILL JENNINGS

(Can't Live Without Your)
LOVE AND AFFECTION
recorded by Nelson
excerpt

Words and Music by MARC TANNER,
MATT NELSON and GUNNAR NELSON

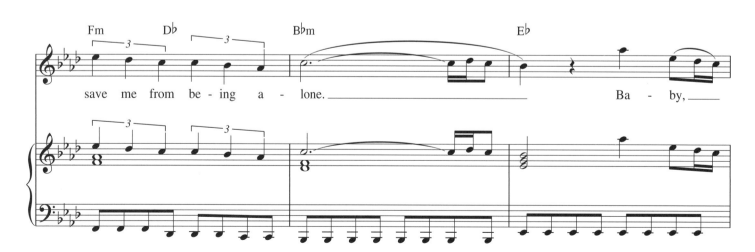

MAYBE I'M AMAZED
recorded by Paul McCartney
excerpt

Words and Music by
PAUL McCARTNEY

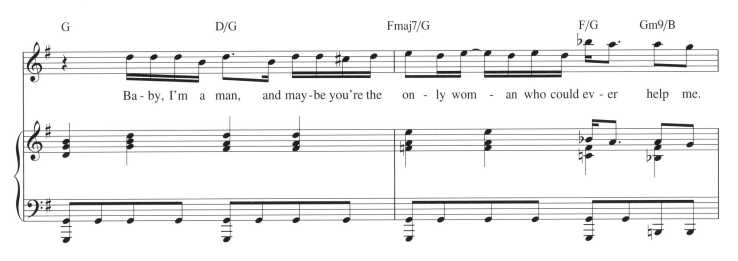

Ba - by, I'm a man, and may - be you're the on - ly wom - an who could ev - er help me.

Ba - by, won't you help me to un - der - stand? ___ Ooh. _____

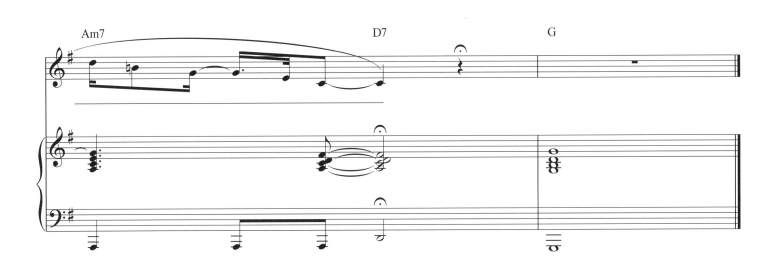

MORE TODAY THAN YESTERDAY

recorded by Spiral Staircase

excerpt

Words and Music by
PAT UPTON

NO MATTER WHAT

from *Whistle down the Wind*

recorded by Boyzone

excerpt

Music by ANDREW LLOYD WEBBER
Lyrics by JIM STEINMAN

No mat-ter who they fol-low, no mat-ter where they lead,

no mat-ter how they judge us, I'll be ev'-ry-one you need. _ I

can't de-ny _ what I _ be-lieve, _ I can't be _ what I'm not.

I know this love's for-ev-er. That's all that mat-ters now no mat-ter what.

NEVER GONNA GIVE YOU UP
recorded by Rick Astley
excerpt

Words and Music by MIKE STOCK,
MATTHEW AITKEN and PETER WATERMAN

Moderate Rock

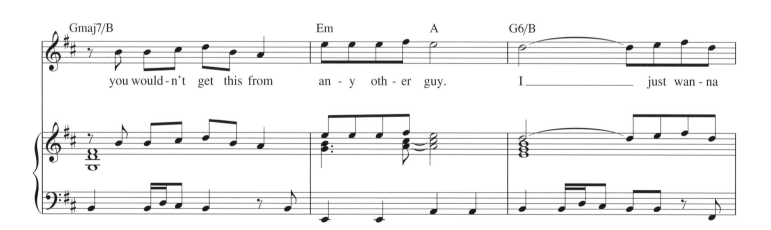

REMEMBER WHEN IT RAINED

recorded by Josh Groban

excerpt

Words and Music by ERIC MOUQUET
and JOSH GROBAN

Lyrics:
Wash a-way the thoughts in-side that keep my mind a-way from you.
No more love and no more pride, and thoughts are all I have to do.

ROCKET MAN
(I Think It's Gonna Be A Long Long Time)
recorded by Elton John
excerpt

Words and Music by ELTON JOHN
and BERNIE TAUPIN

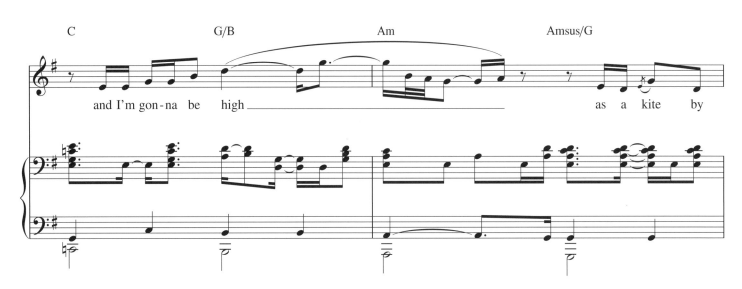

SHE'S ALWAYS A WOMAN
recorded by Billy Joel
excerpt

Words and Music by
BILLY JOEL

Flowing, but accented (♩. = 58)

She can lead you to love. _ She can take you or leave you. She can ask for the truth, _ but she'll nev - er be - lieve _____ you and she'll take what you give her _____ as long as it's free. Yeah, she steals like a thief, _ but she's al-ways a wom-an _____ to me.

SHE'S GOT A WAY

recorded by Billy Joel

excerpt

Words and Music by
BILLY JOEL

Slow and steady (♩ = 72)

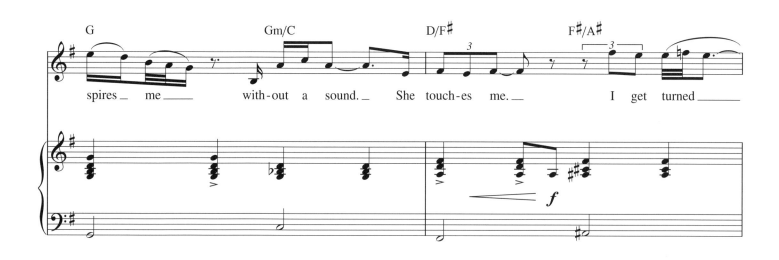

SIGNED, SEALED, DELIVERED I'M YOURS

recorded by Stevie Wonder

excerpt

Words and Music by STEVIE WONDER, SYREETA WRIGHT,
LEE GARRETT and LULA MAE HARDAWAY

Like a fool I went and stayed _ too long. _
Then that time I went and said ___ good-bye. _

Now I'm won - d'rin' if ___ your love's still strong. _ } Ooh, ba - by, here I am, _
Now I'm back _ and not _ a-shamed to cry. ___ }

signed, sealed, de-liv-ered I'm yours. _

SOMETIMES WHEN WE TOUCH

recorded by Dan Hill

excerpt

Words by DAN HILL
Music by BARRY MANN

SOLITAIRE

recorded by Elvis Presley, The Carpenters, Clay Aiken

excerpt

Words and Music by NEIL SEDAKA
and PHIL CODY

Moderately slow

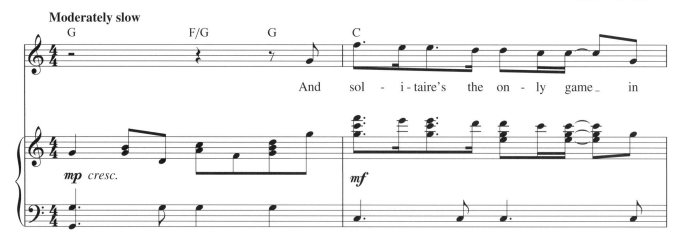

And sol - i - taire's the on - ly game _ in

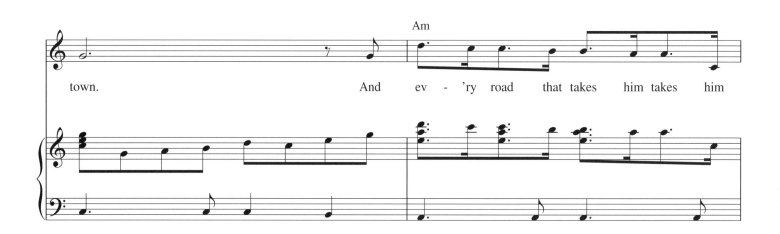

town.   And ev - 'ry road that takes him takes him

down.   And by him - self it's eas - y to pre -

SOMEBODY TO LOVE

recorded by Jefferson Airplane

excerpt

Words and Music by
DARBY SLICK

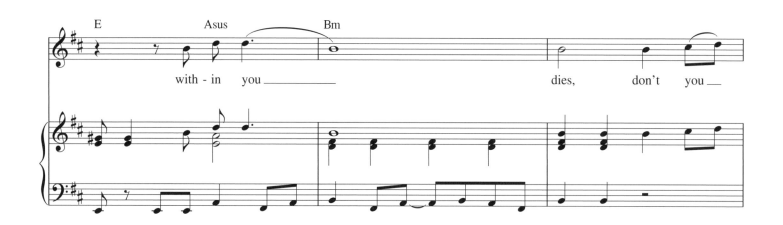

SOMETHING TO TALK ABOUT
(Let's Give Them Something To Talk About)
recorded by Bonnie Raitt
excerpt

Words and Music by
SHIRLEY EIKHARD

We laugh just a lit-tle too loud, ___ we stand ___

___ just a lit-tle too close, ___ we stare ___ just a lit-tle too long. ___

May-be they're see-ing some-thing we don't, dar - ling.

A SONG FOR YOU

recorded by Leon Russell

excerpt

Words and Music by
LEON RUSSELL

Slowly

I've act-ed out my love in stag-es with

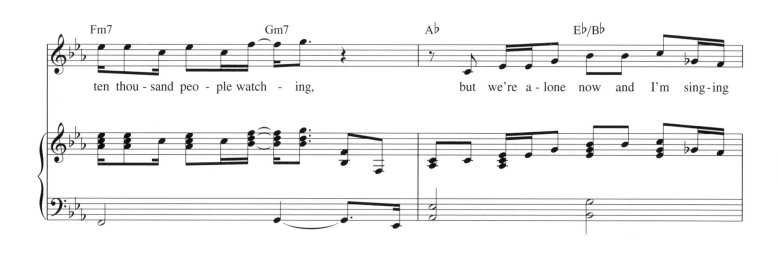

ten thou-sand peo-ple watch-ing, but we're a-lone now and I'm sing-ing

this song for you. I know your im-age of me is what I

SORRY SEEMS TO BE THE HARDEST WORD

recorded by Elton John

excerpt

Words and Music by ELTON JOHN
and BERNIE TAUPIN

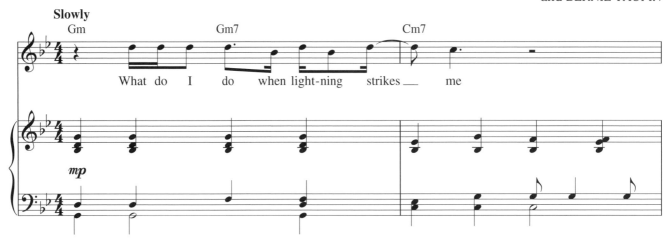

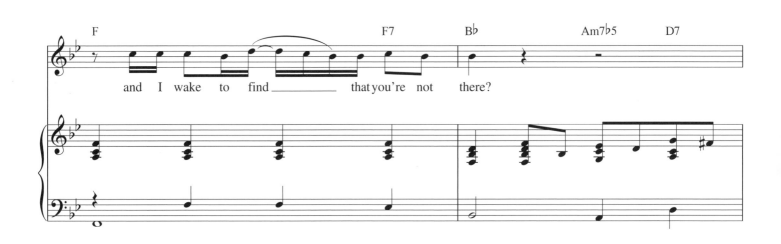

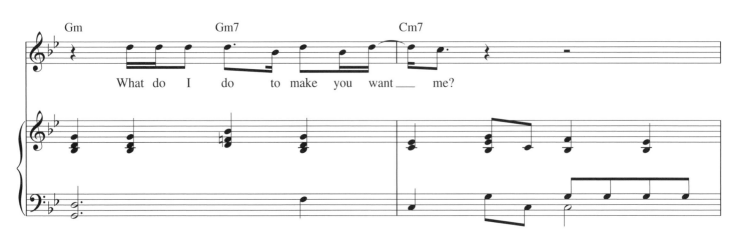

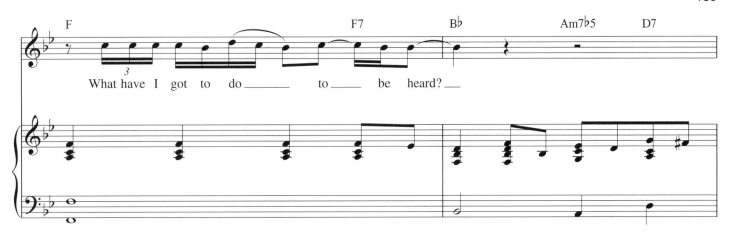

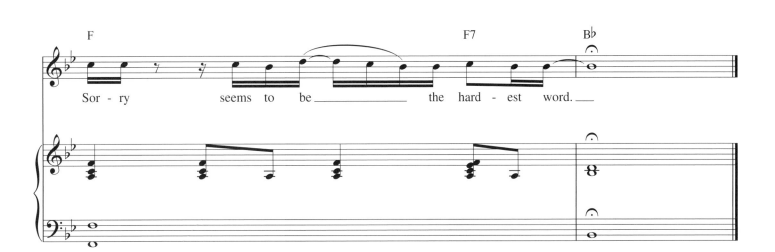

START OF SOMETHING NEW

from the Disney Channel Original Movie *High School Musical*
recorded by Zac Efron and Vanessa Anne Hudgens
excerpt

Words and Music by MATTHEW GERRARD
and ROBBIE NEVIL

WITHOUT YOU
recorded by Badfinger; Mariah Carey

excerpt

Written by PETER HAM
and TOM EVANS

STILL THE SAME
recorded by Bob Seger
excerpt

Words and Music by
BOB SEGER

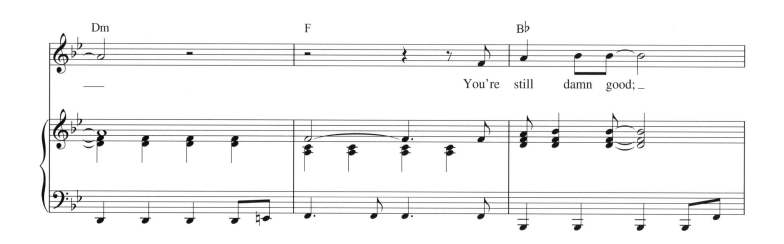

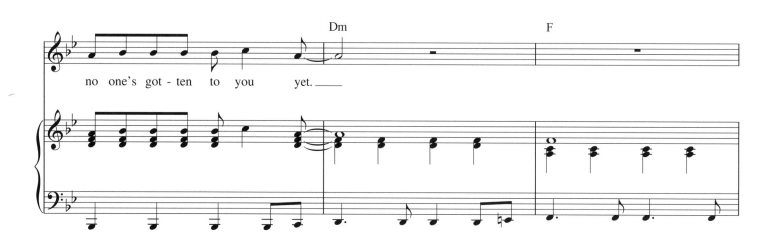

Ev - 'ry time __ they were sure they had you caught, __

you were quick - er than they thought. _____ You'd just turn your back and

walk. __ And you're still the same. __

TAKIN' IT TO THE STREETS

recorded by Michael McDonald

excerpt

Words and Music by
MICHAEL McDONALD

Moderately fast

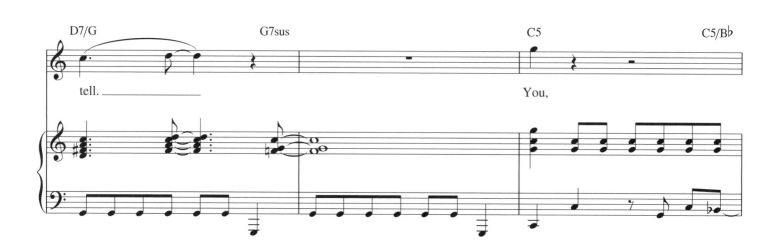

THIS AIN'T A LOVE SONG

recorded by Bon Jovi

excerpt

Words and Music by JON BON JOVI,
RICHIE SAMBORA and DESMOND CHILD

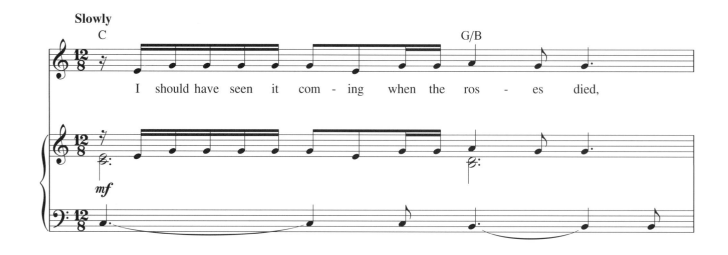

I should have seen it com - ing when the ros - es died,

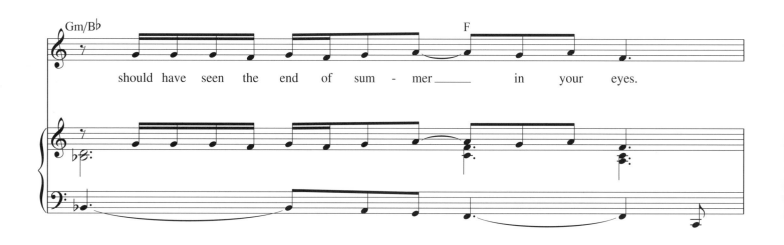

should have seen the end of sum - mer _____ in your eyes.

I should have lis - tened when you said "Good night," You real - ly meant good - bye. ____ I

TINY DANCER

recorded by Elton John

excerpt

Words and Music by ELTON JOHN
and BERNIE TAUPIN

TRAGEDY
recorded by Marc Anthony

excerpt

Words and Music by CORY ROONEY
and ROB THOMAS

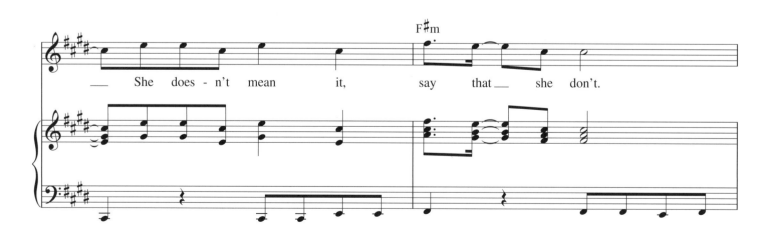

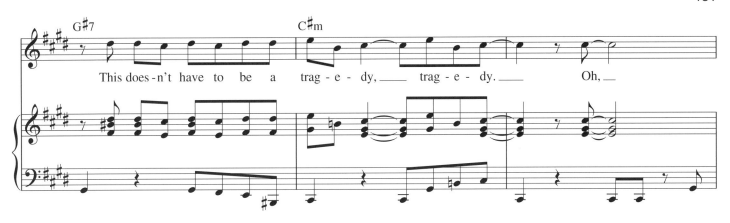

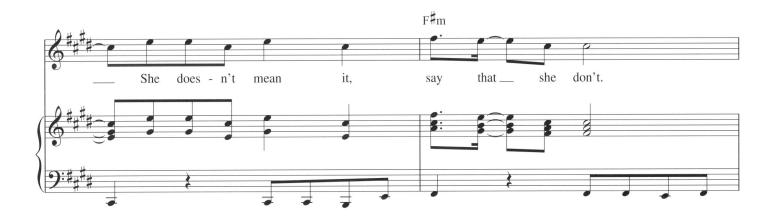

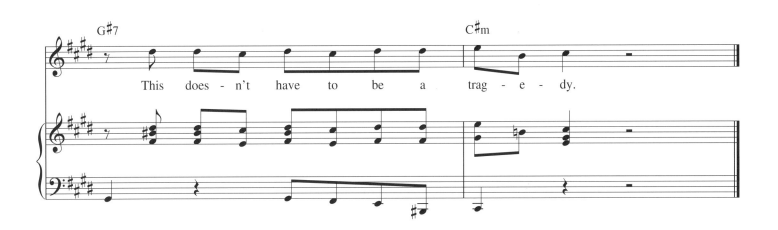

TRUE COLORS
recorded by Cyndi Lauper; Phil Collins
excerpt

Words and Music by BILLY STEINBERG
and TOM KELLY

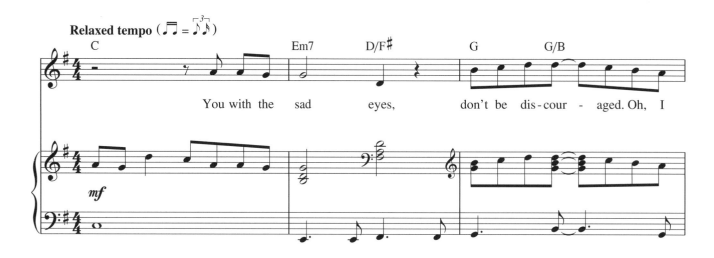

You with the sad eyes, don't be dis-cour-aged. Oh, I

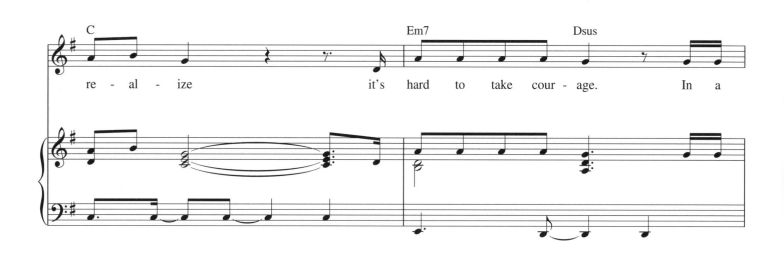

re-al-ize it's hard to take cour-age. In a

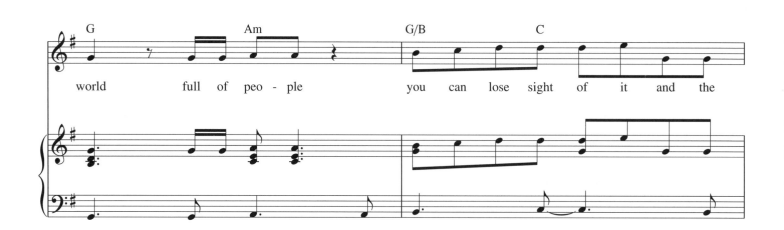

world full of peo-ple you can lose sight of it and the

UNCHAIN MY HEART
recorded by Ray Charles; Joe Cocker
excerpt

Words and Music by BOBBY SHARP
and TEDDY POWELL

WE'VE GOT TONIGHT
recorded by Bob Seger

excerpt

Words and Music by
BOB SEGER

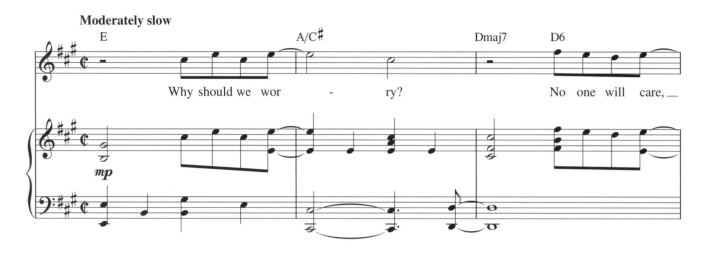

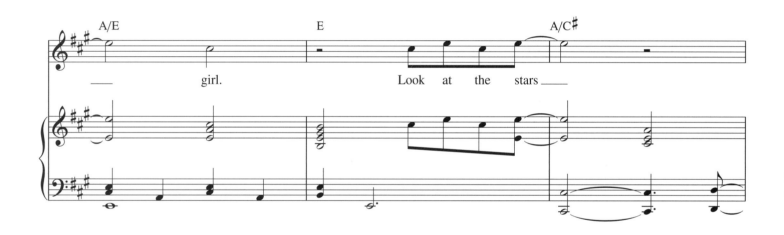

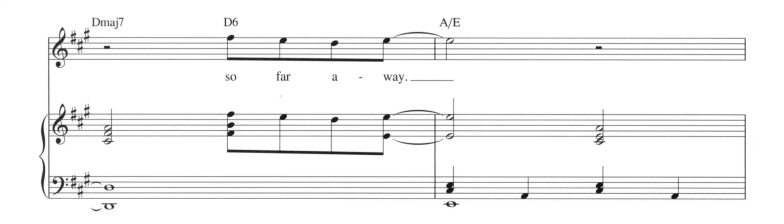

157

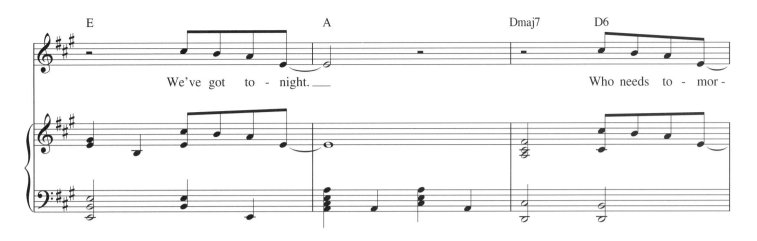

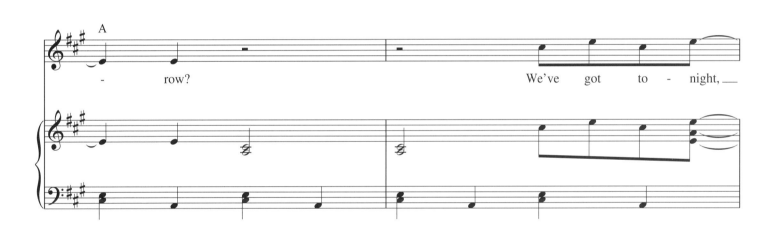

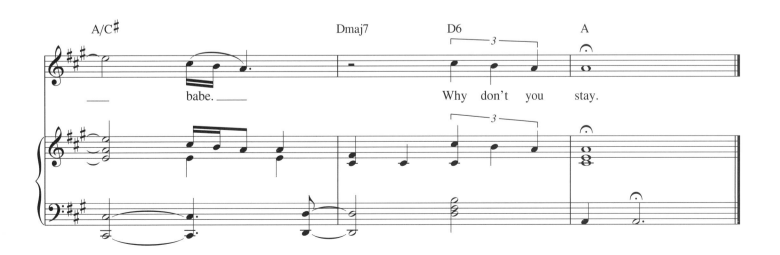

WE'VE ONLY JUST BEGUN

recorded by The Carpenters

excerpt

Words and Music by ROGER NICHOLS
and PAUL WILLIAMS

And yes, we've just be - gun. _____

Shar - ing hor - i - zons that are

new to us, watch - ing the signs a - long the

WILL YOU STILL LOVE ME

recorded by Chicago

excerpt

Words and Music by DAVID FOSTER,
RICHARD BASKIN and TOM KEANE

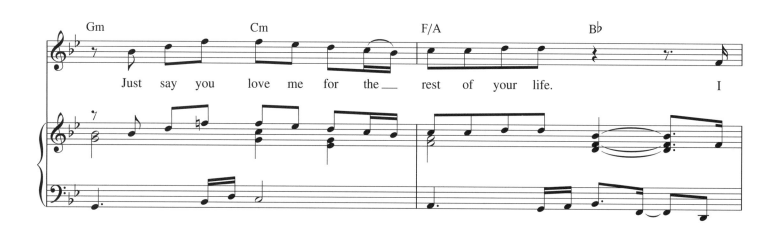

WOULDN'T IT BE NICE

recorded by The Beach Boys

excerpt

Words and Music by BRIAN WILSON,
TONY ASHER and MIKE LOVE

Would-n't it be nice if we were old-er, ___ then ___ we would-n't

have to wait ___ so ___ long ___ and would-n't it be

nice to live to-geth-er ___ in ___ the kind of

YESTERDAY
recorded by The Beatles
excerpt

Words and Music by JOHN LENNON
and PAUL McCARTNEY

Moderately, with expression

Why she had to go I don't

know, she would-n't say. ___ I said

some-thing wrong, now I long for yes-ter-day.

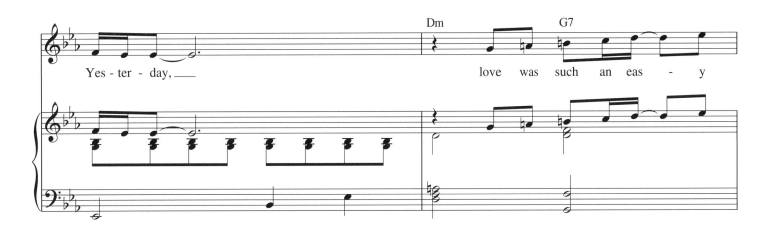

Yes - ter - day, ___ love was such an eas - y

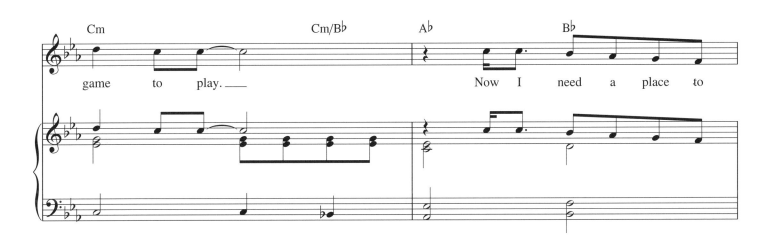

game to play. ___ Now I need a place to

hide a - way, ___ oh I be - lieve ___ in yes - ter - day. ___

YOU ARE SO BEAUTIFUL
recorded by Joe Cocker
excerpt

Words and Music by BILLY PRESTON
and BRUCE FISHER

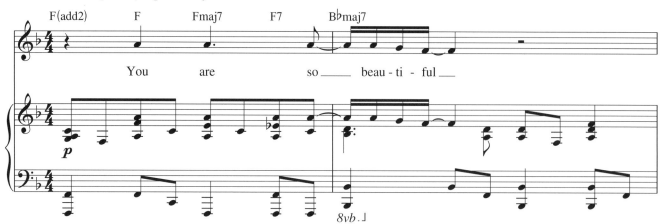

hope for. You're ev-'ry-thing I need. ___

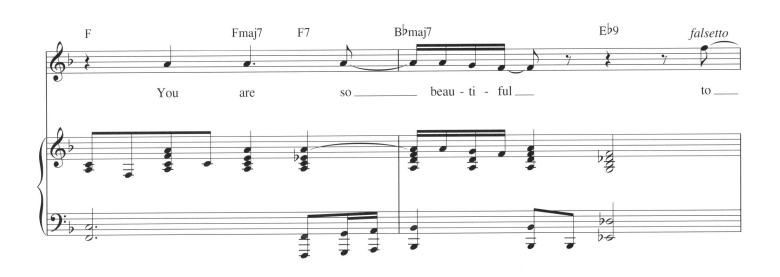

You are so _____ beau-ti-ful ___ to ___

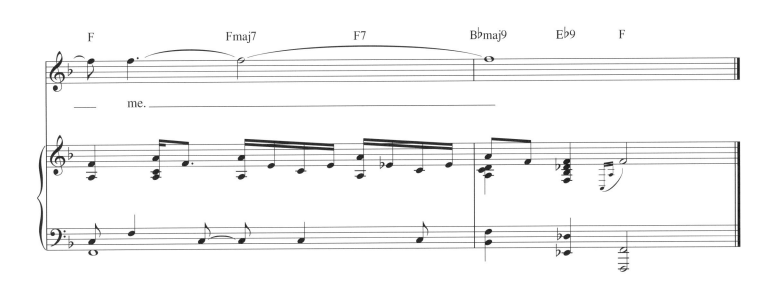

___ me. _____

YOU ARE THE SUNSHINE
OF MY LIFE

recorded by Stevie Wonder

excerpt

Words and Music by
STEVIE WONDER

Moderately, with feeling

I feel like this __ is the __ be - gin - ning, __

'though I've loved you __ for a mil - lion years.

And if I thought __ our love __ was _____ end - ing, __ I'd __ find __

__ my-self __ drown - ing in my __ own tears. Whoa. _____

YOU GIVE LOVE A BAD NAME

recorded by Bon Jovi

excerpt

Words and Music by JON BON JOVI,
DESMOND CHILD and RICHIE SAMBORA

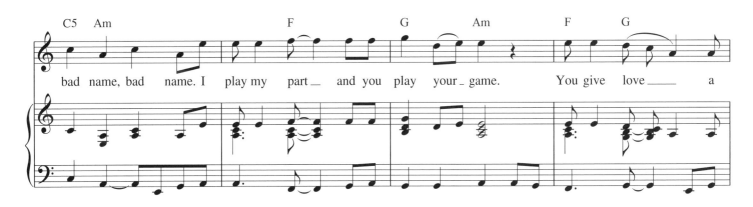

YOU CAN'T HURRY LOVE

recorded by The Supremes; Phil Collins

excerpt

Words and Music by EDWARD HOLLAND,
LAMONT DOZIER and BRIAN HOLLAND

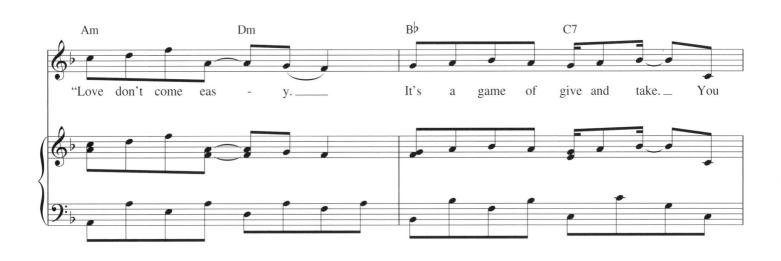

YOU RAISE ME UP
recorded by Josh Groban
excerpt

Words and Music by BRENDAN GRAHAM
and ROLF LOVLAND

When I am down and, oh, my soul's so

wea - ry; when trou - bles come and my heart ___ bur - dened

be; then I am still and wait here in the si - lence un - til ___ You

YOU'LL BE IN MY HEART
(Pop Version)
from Walt Disney Pictures' *Tarzan*™
recorded by Phil Collins
excerpt

Words and Music by
PHIL COLLINS

YOU'RE THE INSPIRATION
recorded by Chicago
excerpt

Words and Music by PETER CETERA
and DAVID FOSTER

Slow Rock

From to-night_ un-til the end_ of time.

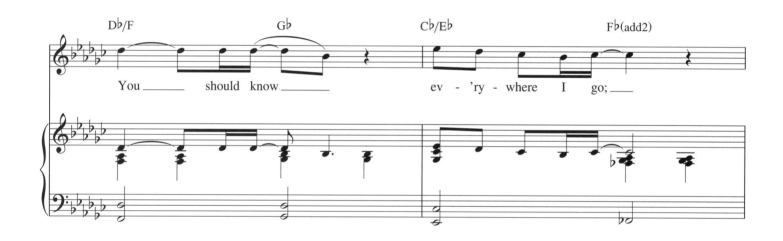

You_ should know_ ev-'ry-where I go;_

al-ways on_ my mind,_ in my heart,_ in my soul,_ ba-by.

YOU'VE LOST THAT LOVIN' FEELIN'

recorded by The Righteous Brothers

excerpt

Words and Music by BARRY MANN,
CYNTHIA WEIL and PHIL SPECTOR

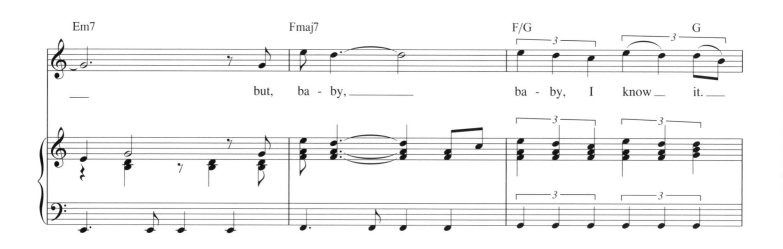

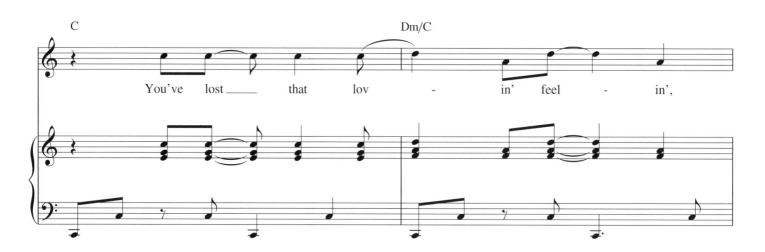

whoa oh, that lov - in' feel - in'.

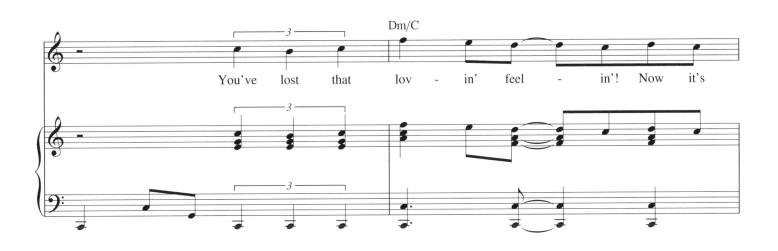

You've lost that lov - in' feel - in'! Now it's

gone, gone, gone, whoa oh oh oh.

YOU'VE MADE ME SO VERY HAPPY

recorded by Blood, Sweat & Tears
excerpt

Words and Music by BERRY GORDY, FRANK E. WILSON,
BRENDA HOLLOWAY and PATRICE HOLLOWAY

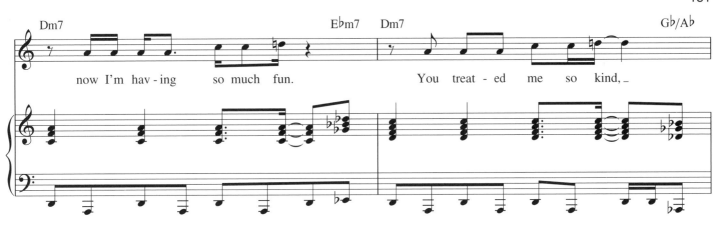

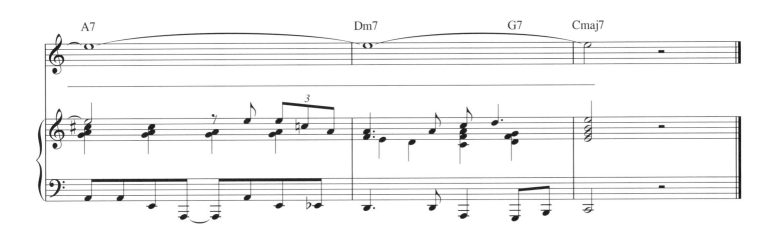

YOUR SONG
recorded by Elton John

excerpt

Words and Music by ELTON JOHN
and BERNIE TAUPIN

Slow Rock Ballad